The GREENLANDERS' SAGA

GEORGE JOHNSTON

Copyright © 1976 by George Johnston

ISBN 0 88750 203 2

Printed in Canada

PUBLISHED IN CANADA BY OBERON PRESS

For Peter

INTRODUCTION

Bjarni Herjulfsson blundered on the New World and did not know where he was. Nor did he seem to care. The story of his discovery spread eastward as far as Denmark but did not make much stir except in Greenland, where Leif Eiriksson bought Bjarni's ship from him and set out to see for himself. Leif found Bjarni's three lands in reverse order, Baffin Land, Labrador and Newfoundland, which he named Flatstone Land, Forest Land and Wineland. He found wild grapes in Wineland and brought grapes, vines and timber home to Greenland; the saga says he brought the grapes home in the spring, so they must have been dry. It says nothing about making wine from them. Leif built dwellings and established a place there, known as Leif's Booths, and stayed a winter. His brother Thorvald then went out in the same ship and wintered there with his crew at Leif's Booths and spent the next summer exploring along the coast of Newfoundland. They wintered again and the following summer explored the Labrador coast and this time they met aborigines, whom they called skraelings. They killed the first skraelings and so stirred up hostility; many of the skraelings attacked their ship and Thorvald was killed by an arrow. He had seen a headland where he had thought he would like to make his steading, and his dying instructions are to bury him there and raise a cross over him. The crew spend the third winter at Leif's Booths and return to Leif in the spring with the heavy news. Wineland has shown its claws.

Two more voyages are made, however. The next one, that of Thorfinn Karlsefni and his wife Gudrid, though it does not establish a settlement, must be considered a prosperous and even illustrious voyage. The saga was probably written in order to tell about it. But it too ends in hostility with skraelings.

The last voyage was a cruel disaster, a moral collapse that brings the Wineland story to a harshly tragic and abrupt end. It is all ugly, even to Leif's uncovering of the truth by means of torture. It is perhaps intended as a contrast to the voyage of Thorfinn Karlsefni and Gudrid, or perhaps it is just the way things happened. The writer tells it grimly, and it seems to mark the end of the Norse western thrust.

The Greenlanders' Saga is hardly a tale of New World discovery. It tells about farmers and merchants who had good ships and were skilful in sailing and navigating them. They cross hazardous open seas but never as if they were venturing on a wide ocean with an unknown or only guessed-at far shore. Instead they seem to follow a coastline as long as they think it is worth following. The furthest land they reach looks promising at first, but its promise turns sour, and so far as we know they gave up efforts to settle it.

Two sagas tell of the chain of events I have outlined, with some differences. In this summary I have followed *The Greenlanders' Saga*. In *Eirik the Red's Saga*, which is a more consciously literary telling, Leif is the one who

6

comes by accident on the New World, and there is no mention of Bjarni Herjulfsson; furthermore, the four voyages of *The Greenlanders' Saga* are conflated to two and the naming of the countries is given to Thorfinn Karlsefni instead of Leif. Thorvald is on Karlsefni's expedition, and the arrow that kills him is shot by a uniped, a marvellous creature who seems to belong to the travel literature of the time, along with unicorns, basilisks, anthropophagi and such creatures of the mediaeval imagination. Supernatural incidents, such as the deaths of Thorstein and Grimhild, or the appearance of Gudrid's namesake in Wineland, or the charming story of the Greenland Spae-wife, do not interfere with the tone of sober history, set especially by *The Greenlanders' Saga*, but the uniped in *Eirik the Red's Saga* seems to come from a different kind of literature.

The sagas cannot both be right about the order of the voyages, and no evidence has come to light that will decide in favour of either. In a now-famous article the Icelandic scholar, the late Dr. Jón Jóhannesson, put forward strong arguments to prove that *The Greenlanders' Saga* is not only older than *Eirik the Red's Saga* but also the source for much of its material. Olafur Halldórsson, however, now thinks that the sagas were written independently of one another at the beginning of the thirteenth century, and had a shared source in stories handed down. Geoffrey Gathorne-Hardy, a thoughtful and reasonable writer on the subject of the Norsemen in America, prefers the story of Bjarni's discovery. "I submit," says he, "that we have here a very clear and correct account of the way

7

in which America was discovered, whether by Bjarni or another." And for many readers the bare account given by the writer of *The Greenlanders' Saga*, with its interest in craft and technical details, will seem the more authentic. If this is not history, one feels, it must be as close to it as the writer could get. Yet there are discrepancies in the story. Why did Bjarni go to Earl Eirik's court, after he had quit sailing, and tell his story there? And why did the talk about his discovery then come up, apparently for the first time, in Greenland? Olafur Halldórsson suggests that in the original saga Bjarni had told his story to Eirik the Red, and that Earl Eirik's name had been substituted for his between the composition of the saga and its copying-out into the *Flateyjarbók* a hundred years or so later. Someone along the way had tried to make sense of the two facts, that Bjarni was a retainer of Earl Eirik, and had also told an Eirik about unplanned discoveries on his way to Greenland, and had not noticed the discrepancies involved.

In summarizing the story I have assumed that Leif's Booths were at L'Anse-aux-Meadows at the northern tip of Newfoundland, where Helge and Anne Stine Ingstad uncovered the only known archaeological evidence to date of the Norse presence in North America. That this was the place mentioned in the saga is still not sure, but it makes geographical and literary sense, and I have based my summary on it.

The Greenlanders' Saga was interpolated in two parts into *The Great Saga of Olaf Tryggvason* as it was copied into *Flateyjarbók* at the end of the fourteenth century.

Flateyjarbók, or in English *The Flat-Island Book*, so named after Flat Island in Broad Firth in West Iceland, where its seventeenth-century owners lived, is one of the most famous and beautiful and also the largest of the Norse manuscript treasures. It is a compilation made up chiefly of the sagas of Olaf Tryggvason and Olaf the Saint, into which were interpolated, besides *The Greenlanders' Saga*, the sagas of the Jomsvikings, of the Orkney Islanders, of the Faroe Islanders, *Hallfred's Saga*, *The Foster-Brothers' Saga* and others. Besides the two sagas of Olaf there were also *Sverri's Saga* and *The Saga of Hakon Hakonarson*. The sagas of Magnus the Good and Harald the Stern were added in the fifteenth century. The book was given in 1647 to Bishop Brynjolf Sveinsson, who then gave it to King Frederik III of Denmark, and it remained in the Royal Library in Copenhagen until it was moved recently to Reykjavík. It is now in the care of the University of Iceland.

In this translation I have followed the text in Olafur Halldórsson's new edition of *Grænlandinga saga*, which was published in Reykjavík in *Grænlands annál* in 1975. The original beginning of the saga has been lost and this edition begins with the account of Bjarni Herjulfsson's voyage. Short passages from *Islendingabók (Book of the Icelanders)* and *Landnámabók (Book of the Settlements)* —edited by Jakob Benediktsson, *Islenzk fornrit* I. 13-14 *(Islendingabók)* and 130-132, 134 *(Landnámabók)*— telling of Eirik the Red's settlement is given after the text of the saga as an appendix. In making the translation I have followed my usual practice, which is to keep close

9

to the Icelandic and echo in my style so far as possible its vocabulary, sentence structure and rhythms. I have wanted to keep the plain, serious style of this author, which I admire, and the sense that he is telling, as truthfully as he can, what happened.

Peter Foote was the first to look over this translation, and now as heretofore I have been greatly helped by the generosity of his scholarship and his fine sense of style. Richard Perkins knows the Wineland story well, and he was friendly and enthusiastic in sharing his insights. He and Olafur Halldórsson looked over the manuscript at a late stage, and what authority it has is owing largely to their care, though they cannot, of course, be responsible for the final text, with many points of which they may not agree. In many passages I was happy to be able to consult Hans Bekker-Nielsen's Danish version of the saga, which he prepared for the exhibition, *Erik den Rødes Grønland*, Copenhagen, 1967. Besides providing an authoritative text and reading over my manuscript, Olafur Halldórsson has been generous with new information, and his own very interesting insights into small dramas in the story. His help has been invaluable in pulling this little edition into shape.

The
GREENLANDERS' SAGA

CHAPTER I

Herjulf was the son of Bard Herjulfsson. Herjulf the elder was kinsman of Ingolf the Settler. To Herjulf and his son, Ingolf gave land between Vag and Reykjaness.

Herjulf Bardsson settled first at Drepstokk. Thorgerd was his wife and Bjarni their son, and he was a most promising man. He was keen to go abroad when he was still young, and did well by it, both in wealth and fame, and he was turn about, winter by winter, overseas or at home with his father. Bjarni soon had his own ship trading. And during his last winter in Norway, then Herjulf joined the Greenland voyage with Eirik and gave up his farm. With Herjulf on his ship was a Hebridean, a Christian, the man who composed the Seaquake poem. In it is this stanza:

> I pray the spotless monk-prover
> prevail for me in my sailing;
> Holy Master of high Heaven's
> Hall, may his hawk's perch follow me.

Herjulf settled at Herjulf's Ness; he was a most noble man.

Eirik the Red settled at Brattahlid. He was held in greatest esteem there, and all deferred to him. These were Eirik's children: Leif, Thorvald and Thorstein, and Freydis was his daughter; she was married to the man Thorvard, and they lived at Gardar, where the bishop's seat

12

is now. She was a very high-handed woman and Thorvard was nothing much; she was mostly married for money.

The Greenland folk were heathen then.

That same summer Bjarni brought his ship in at Eyrar, after his father had sailed away in the spring. Bjarni was amazed by the news, and would not unload his ship. His crew asked him what he meant to do, and he answers that he meant to follow his way and take his winter's keep from his father—"and I want to sail on to Greenland, if you will stay with me."

All declared that they wanted to do as he said.

Then Bjarni spoke: "Reckless our trip will seem, since none of us has ever sailed into the Greenland sea."

Nevertheless they stand out to sea as soon as they were ready, and sailed for three days, until the land had sunk under the skyline behind them, and then the good wind failed and northerly breezes and fog came up, and they did not know which way they were going, and so it went on for many days.

After that they saw the sun and then they could tell which way they were going; then they let out their sail and go on for a day before they saw land, and wondered among themselves what land that might be, and Bjarni says he thinks it is not Greenland.

They ask whether he wants to sail close to this land or not. "It is my plan to sail in close to the land."

They do so, and soon saw that the land was not mountainous and it was wooded, and small hills were in the land, and they kept the land to port and sailed close-hauled along it.

Then on they went for two days' sailing before they saw another land.

They ask whether Bjarni thought it was Greenland this time.

He said he thought this no more Greenland than the first—"because the glaciers are said to be mighty big in Greenland."

They came straight in towards this land and saw that it was a flat land and had trees growing on it. Then their wind failed them. The crew all agreed that it would be a good plan to go ashore, but Bjarni did not want this. They reckoned they were in need of both wood and water.

"You are not short of these at all," says Bjarni, but even so he got mutterings about this from his crew.

He told them to let out the sail, and this was done, and they swung the prow seawards and sailed away in a south-west wind for three days' sailing, and saw a third land then; and it was high and mountainous and there were glaciers on it.

Then they ask if Bjarni wanted to go ashore there, and he said he did not want to—"because to me this land seems unpromising."

They did not haul in their sail; they follow along the coast and saw that it was an island; swung the prow from land again and stood out to sea in the same wind. But the wind stiffened and then Bjarni ordered the sail reefed and said they were not to run harder than ship and rigging would easily stand; then they go on for four days' sailing.

Then they saw a fourth land. They asked Bjarni whether he reckoned this would be Greenland or not.

Bjarni answers: "This is most like what has been told me of Greenland, and we shall make for shore here."

They do so, and come in at a ness late in the afternoon, and there was a boat hauled up on the ness. And here lived Herjulf, Bjarni's father, on the ness, and from him the ness has taken its name and has since been called Herjulf's Ness. Bjarni went to his father, and he quits voyaging now and stays with his father as long as Herjulf lived. And then he carried on farming there after his father.

CHAPTER II

Next thing to be told is that Bjarni Herjulfsson came out from Greenland and went to see Earl Eirik Hakonsson, and the Earl received him well. Bjarni told about his voyage when he had seen the lands, and everyone thought he had been pretty uncurious, since he had nothing to tell about those lands, and for this he got some criticism.

Bjarni became a retainer of the Earl and went out to Greenland the following summer. There was much talk now about exploring.

Leif, son of Eirik the Red of Brattahlid, went to see Bjarni Herjulfsson and bought the ship from him and got a crew for it, so that there were 35 men altogether. Leif asked his father Eirik if he would once again be in command of the voyage.

Eirik rather wanted to beg off, said he was getting on in age and said he was less able to put up with all the hardships than he used to be. Leif said that there was most luck with him still, of all the kinsmen. So Eirik gave in to Leif and he rides out when they were about ready, and it was not far to go to the ship. The horse stumbled that Eirik was riding, and he was thrown and hurt his leg. Then Eirik spoke: "It is not meant for me to discover more lands than this, which we live in now. Our faring together is over." Eirik went home to Brattahlid, and Leif went aboard his ship and his men with him, 35 in all. There was a German on the voyage who was called Tyrkir.

Now they readied their ship and put to sea when they were ready, and came upon the land first that Bjarni and his crew had seen last. They sailed up to the land and cast anchor and launched their boat and rowed ashore and saw no grass there. Great glaciers were all the higher part, and it was like one flat rock all the way to the glaciers from the sea, and to them this land looked barren.

Then Leif spoke: "It has not turned out for us at this land as for Bjarni, that we did not go ashore. I shall give a name to this land and call it Flatstone Land."

Then back they went to the ship.

After this they stand out to sea and came upon a second land; once again they sail up to the land and cast anchor, launch the boat and go ashore. This land was flat and wooded, and white sand in many places, and sloping gently to the sea.

16

Then Leif spoke: "By its worth shall this land be named, and called Forest Land." Then they went right back out to their ship.

From there they stand out to sea in a northeast wind and were out for two days' sailing before they saw land, and sailed for the land and reached an island that lay to the north offshore, and climbed up on it and looked about in the fine weather, and found that there was dew on the grass, and it happened that they got their hands into the dew and brought it to their mouths and it seemed as though they had not tasted anything so sweet as that was.

Then they went back to their ship and sailed into the sound that lay between the island and the ness that stretched northward from the land; they steered a westerly course around the ness. There was a wide shallow at the ebb and their ship stranded, but there was still a long reach of sea to be seen from the ship.

But they had such a curiosity to go ashore that they would not wait until the tide came up under their ship, and they ran ashore at a place where a river flowed out of a lake. And when the tide came up under their ship they took their boat and rowed to the ship and towed it up into the river, and then into the lake, and anchored there and took their bed-sacks ashore and put up shelters there; made up their minds then to stay there over the winter, and built a big house.

There was no dearth of salmon, either in the river or in the lake, and bigger salmon than they had ever seen before.

Living was so good there, as it seemed to them, that

they would need no fodder for cattle in winter; there was no frost in winter and the grass hardly withered. Days and nights were more of a length than in Greenland or Iceland; the sun had mid-morning and mid-afternoon there on the shortest day.

And when they had finished their building, then Leif spoke with his men: "Now I want to have our crew divided in two, and have the land explored, and one part of the crew is to stay at home by the house, and the other part is to explore the country but not go further than they can get back home from by dusk, and not separate."

Now they carried on this way for a while. Leif was turn about, that he went with the explorers, or was at home at the house.

Leif was a big strong man, a most manly man to look at, a wise and good man and a moderate man in all things.

CHAPTER III

One evening this was the news, that a man was missing of their crew, and it was Tyrkir the German. Leif was very grieved over this because Tyrkir had been in his father's household a long while and had been fond of Leif as a child. Leif blamed his men sorely and got ready to go out to find him, and twelve men with him.

But they had hardly got away from the house when

18

there came Tyrkir towards them, and they were glad to see him.

Leif soon found that his foster-father was in good spirits. He was a stiff-necked and quick-eyed man, small-featured, not tall, rather undergrown, and yet a skilled man in all sorts of crafts.

Then Leif spoke to him: "Why were you so slow, my foster-father, and away from all the rest?"

At first he spoke in German for a long while and darted his eyes every way and grinned. But they could not understand what he was saying.

Then he began to speak in Norse after a while: "I had not gone much further than you. I know something new to tell: I found grape-vines and grapes."

"Can that be true, my foster-father?" said Leif.

"For sure it is true," said he, "for I was brought up where there was no dearth of grape-vines or grapes."

They slept over it that night, and in the morning Leif said to his crew: "From now on we shall have two tasks, every other day to each: gather grapes or cut vines, and fell timber, and so make the cargo of my ship." And this was what they did.

It is said that their cock-boat was full of grapes.

Then a cargo of timber was cut for the ship.

And when spring comes, then they got ready and sailed away, and Leif named the land for what it grew and called it Wineland. Now they stand out to sea, and there was a good wind for them all the way till they came in sight of Greenland and its mountains under the ice.

Then one man spoke and said to Leif: "Why are you

bringing the ship up so close to the wind?"

Leif answered: "My mind is on my steering, but it is on something else too, and what do you see that is new?"

They said they saw nothing that could be called news.

"I cannot be sure," says Leif, "whether I see a ship or a skerry."

They see it now, and said it was a skerry. His sight was sharper than theirs, for he made out men on the skerry.

"Now I want us to beat up against the wind," says Leif, "so that we can come up to them, in case they need us and there is some help to be given them; and if it turns out that they are not peaceful men, then we have all the advantage on our side and they have none."

Now they fetch up by the skerry and lowered their sail, cast anchor and launched a second little boat that they had with them.

Then Leif asked them who was in charge of their crew.

He says he is called Thorir, and a Norwegian by birth. "And what is your name?"

Leif tells who he is.

"Are you the son of Eirik the Red of Brattahlid?" says he.

Leif says he is. "And I am willing," says Leif, "to take you all on my ship and as much of your goods as the ship will hold."

They took this offer, and then they sailed on into Eirik's Firth with the cargo, and on til they came to Brattahlid; unloaded the cargo from the ship. Leif then offered Thorir winter quarters with him, and Gudrid his wife, and three other men, and got winter quarters for the other

crew, both Thorir's men and his. Leif took fifteen men
from the skerry. He was ever after that called Leif the
Lucky.

Leif was now well off and greatly honoured.

That winter a bad disease hit Thorir and his crew, and
Thorir died and many of his crew. That winter Eirik the
Red died too.

Now there was much talk about Leif's Wineland voyage, and it seemed to Thorvald, his brother, that the land
had been far too little explored. Then Leif spoke with
Thorvald: "Off you go in my ship, brother, if you want
to, to Wineland, but I want the ship first to get Thorir's
timber off the skerry."

And so it was done.

CHAPTER IV

Now Thorvald got ready for this voyage with 30 men,
under the direction of Leif his brother. Then they readied
their ship and stood out to sea, and nothing is told of their
voyage before they reach Wineland at Leif's Booths, and
laid up their ship and did not stir over the winter and
caught fish to eat.

And in the spring Thorvald said they must put their
ship in order, and that the ship's boat with some men in it
should go westward around the shore and explore there

during the summer. The country seemed beautiful to them and well wooded, and not much land between the shore and the woods, and white beaches. It was thick with islands there, and much shallow water.

They found no men's houses nor any animals. But on an island farther west they came on a grain barn made of wood. They found no other trace of man's hand, and they came back and arrived at Leif's Booths in the fall.

And the next summer Thorvald took the ship eastward and then north around the coast. Then a gale struck them, off a headland, and drove them ashore there, and smashed the keel under the ship and they had a long hold-up there and repaired their ship. Then Thorvald spoke with his crew: "Now I want us to stand this keel up on the headland here and call it Keel Ness." And so they did.

Then they put out from there and eastward along the shore and into the jaws of a firth nearby and up to the headland that jutted out there. It was all wooded. Then they bring up their ship and run gang-planks ashore and Thorvald goes up on the land with all his men.

Then he spoke: "It is beautiful here, and here is where I would build my farm." Then they go to the ship, and they see across the dunes in from the headland three humps, and they went over and saw three skin boats there and three men under each. Then they divided their force and seized them all, only one got away with his boat. They kill the other eight and go back up on the headland and looked about and saw humps further in the firth, and reckoned that people would be living there.

After that such a heaviness came on them that they could not stay awake, and they all fall asleep. Then a voice called to them and they all woke up; here is what the voice says: "Wake up, Thorvald, and all your men, if you want to stay alive, and get to your ship, you and all your men, and pull away from land as quickly as you can."

Then down the firth came hundreds of skin boats and made for them.

Then Thorvald spoke: "We must get wattle on board and shelter as well as we can, but hardly fight back."

So they do, and the skraelings shot at them for a while, and then flee away as fast as they could, each a different way.

Then Thorvald asked his men if they were wounded at all; they said they were not wounded. "I have got a wound under my arm," says he, "for an arrow came between the gunwale and my shield and in under my arm, and here is the arrow, and this will be my death. Now I advise you to get ready to go back as quickly as you can the way you came, and me you must take to the headland that I thought was so good for a farm. It may be that the truth was on my tongue, that I should dwell there for a while. There you must bury me and put crosses at my head and feet, and call that headland Cross Ness from now on."

Greenland had become Christian then, though Eirik the Red had died before Christianity.

Now Thorvald died and they did everything as he had told them, and then they went back and got to the rest of their company, and each party told the other what news they had, and they wintered there and gathered grapes and vines for their ship's cargo.

Then they get ready in the spring to leave and go back to Greenland, and brought their ship into Eirik's Firth, and for Leif they had heavy news to tell.

CHAPTER V

It happened meanwhile in Greenland that Thorstein of Eirik's Firth had got married, to Gudrid Thorbjorn's daughter, who had been married to the Norwegian Thorir who has already been told about.

Now Thorstein Eiriksson is keen to go to Wineland for the body of Thorvald his brother, and he got the same ship ready and chose a crew of tall strong men and had 25 men with him and Gudrid his wife, and they sail out to sea when they are ready, and out of sight of land. They were blown about all summer and did not know what way they were going.

And when it was a week before winter, then they at last came to land in Lysu Firth in Greenland, in the Western Settlement. Thorstein looked for keep and got keep for all his crew. But he was without a place to stay, and his wife. So they two stayed by the ship for some nights. Christianity was then still new in Greenland.

Then one day men came to their tent early. The one

who was chief among them asked what people were in the tent.

Thorstein answers: "Two people," says he; "but who is asking?"

"My name is Thorstein and I am called Thorstein the Black. And this is my errand here, that I want to offer to have you two, man and wife, to stay with me."

Thorstein says that he wants his wife's decision, but she told him to decide, and then he says yes.

"Then I shall come and get you both tomorrow, with a cart, for I lack nothing to look after you, but it is a lonely life to be with me, two of us are the household there, because I am a very lone kind of man. Another faith I hold than the one you have, and yet I think that is better, that you have."

Then he came after them next day with a cart, and they went to stay with Thorstein the Black, and he kept them well.

Gudrid was a handsome woman to look at, and a wise woman, and she knew well how to get along with strangers.

It was early in the winter that disease hit Thorstein Eiriksson's men and many of his crew died there.

Thorstein had coffins made for the bodies of those who had died, and had them taken to the ship and kept there —"because I want to have all the bodies moved to Eirik's Firth in the summer."

There is not long to wait then until the disease reaches Thorstein's household, and his wife took sick first, Grimhild by name. She was a great big woman and strong as a man, but just the same the disease laid her low. And soon after that the disease took Thorstein Eiriksson, and he and Grimhild were down with it at the same time, and Grimhild died, Thorstein the Black's wife.

And when she was dead, then out went Thorstein from the hearth-room after a board for laying the body on.

Gudrid spoke then: "Do not be away for long, my Thorstein," says she.

He said he would not.

Then Thorstein Eiriksson spoke: "There is something queer about what our housewife is doing, because here she is now, sitting up on her elbow and putting her feet out from the bed and groping about for her shoes."

And in comes Farmer Thorstein and Grimhild falls back down at this, whereupon every beam creaked in the room.

Now Thorstein makes a coffin for Grimhild's body and carried her away to bury her. He was a big man and strong, but he needed all he had before he got her out of the house.

Then the fever grew worse in Thorstein Eiriksson, and he died. Gudrid, his wife, took this hard. They were then all in the hearth-room. Gudrid had been sitting in a chair in front of the bench where he had been lying, Thorstein, her husband.

Then Farmer Thorstein picked Gudrid up from the chair in his arms, and sat on another bench with her, across from the body of Thorstein, and talked with her this way and that way and comforted her, and promised her this, that he would go with her to Eirik's Firth with the body of Thorstein her husband, and the bodies of his men. "And I shall get more of a household up here to comfort and cheer you."

She thanked him.

Thorstein Eiriksson then sat up and spoke: "Where is Gudrid?"

Three times he said this, but she kept mum.

Then she spoke to farmer Thorstein: "Which shall I do, answer him or not?"

He told her not to answer. Then farmer Thorstein went across the floor and sat down in the chair and Gudrid sat on his knee.

And then farmer Thorstein spoke: "What is it that you want, namesake?" says he.

He answers, after a while: "This is my wish, to tell Gudrid her fate, so that she may then better take my death, for I have come to a good resting place. And this is to be told to you, Gudrid, that you will be married to an Icelander, and long will be your life together, and many men will be descended from you two, splendid men, illustrious and famous, sweet and of a good savour. You and your husband shall go from Greenland to Norway, and from there to Iceland, and settle in Iceland. There you two shall live long, and you longer than he. You shall depart again and make the Rome pilgrimage and then come back out to Iceland to your farm, and then a church will have been built there, and you shall live there and become a nun, and there you shall die."

And then Thorstein falls back, and his body was laid out and taken to the ship.

Farmer Thorstein faithfully did everything for Gudrid that he had promised. He sold his land in the spring, and his livestock, and he went to the ship with Gudrid, and with all his possessions, got the ship ready and manned it and then sailed off to Eirik's Firth. The bodies were then buried in the churchyard.

Gudrid went to Leif's in Brattahlid, but Thorstein the Black made himself a steading in Eirik's Firth and stayed there for the rest of his life, and he was thought to be a most manly man.

CHAPTER VI

That same summer a ship arrived from Norway in Greenland. The man was Thorfinn Karlsefni who captained the ship. He was the son of Thord Horse-head, Snorri's son, who was the son of Thord of Hofdi.

Thorfinn Karlsefni was a very rich man and stayed the winter at Brattahlid with Leif Eiriksson. At once he took a liking to Gudrid and asked for her hand, and she asked Leif to answer for her. Then she was betrothed to him and their bridal feast was celebrated that winter.

There was the same talk about the Wineland voyage as before, and people urged Karlsefni to make it, Gudrid no less than others. So then he undertook the voyage, and got a crew together, 60 men and 5 women.

They made this agreement between them, Karlsefni
and his crew, that they would share and share alike all
goods that they might get. They had all kinds of livestock with them because they meant to begin a settlement
if they could.

Karlsefni asked Leif for his buildings in Wineland,
and he said he would lend the buildings, but not give
them.

Then they stood their ship out to sea and reached Leif's
Booths safe and sound, and took ashore their bed-sacks.
Right at hand for them was a big take of food, and good,
for a red whale was stranded there, a good big one; out
they went then and cut it up; then they were not short of
food. The livestock were brought ashore, and it was not
long till the ungelded beasts became lively and unruly.
They had brought a bull with them.

Karlsefni had timber felled and hewn for a cargo, and
the boards laid on rock to season. They made full use of
the land's goods, whatever was there, grapes and all kinds
of game and fish and other good things.

After that first winter came summer. Then they were
aware of skraelings, and out of the woods came a crowd
of men. It was near the cattle, and the bull took to roaring
and bellowing with a terrible noise. This frightened the
skraelings and away they went with what they were car-
rying, which was grey furs and sable and all kinds of pelts,
and they came round to Karlsefni's steading and wanted
to get into the house, but Karlsefni had the door held
against them. Neither understood the other's speech.

Then the skraelings put their bundles down and undid

29

them and offered them, and wanted weapons for them rather than anything else, but Karlsefni banned the bartering of weapons.

And now he tries out a plan of this kind, and told the women to bring out milk for them, and as soon as they saw the milk they wanted that and nothing else. So the skraelings' bargain was this, that they carried their goods away in their stomachs, and Karlsefni and his men had the bundles they left, and the pelts. With this they went away.

Next thing to tell is that Karlsefni had a stout stockade raised around the buildings, and made it tight. At that time a son was born to Gudrid, Karlsefni's wife, and this son was named Snorri. At the onset of the next winter the skraelings came to trade with them and many more than before, and had the same goods as before.

Then Karlsefni spoke to the women: "Now you must bring out the food that was so sought after last time, and nothing else."

And when they saw this they threw their bundles in over the stockade. And Gudrid was sitting in the doorway inside by the cradle of Snorri, her son. Then a shadow fell across the doorway, and in came a woman in a black kirtle, rather short, and had a fillet around her head and light chestnut hair, pale-faced and big-eyed, such big eyes as have never been seen in a human head.

She went towards where Gudrid sat and spoke: "What is your name?" says she.

"My name is Gudrid; now, what is your name?"

"My name is Gudrid," says she.

Then housewife Gudrid beckoned to her that she should sit beside her, and then it happened all at once that Gudrid heard a great crash, and the woman had vanished, and just then also a skraeling was killed by one of Karlsefni's hands, because he had tried to make off with some of their weapons, and they fled then as fast as they could, and their clothing got left behind, and what they had brought. Nobody had seen the woman except only Gudrid.

"Now we have to decide what to do," says Karlsefni, "because I reckon that they will pay us a third visit and not peacefully, and in large numbers. Now this is the plan we shall follow, that ten men are to go out onto the headland and show themselves there, and another group of us shall go into the woods and hew a clearing there for our livestock, for when the skraelings come out of the woods again, and we shall catch our bull and drive him out ahead of us."

And it was like this where they meant to confront the skraelings that there was the lake on one side and woods on the other. This plan was held to, that Karlsefni had put forward.

Now up came the skraelings to the place which Karlsefni meant for the fight. Then the fight began and many skraelings were killed.

One man was big and handsome in the skraeling troop, and it seemed to Karlsefni that he must be their chieftain.

Now one of the skraelings had picked up an axe and looked at it for a bit and swung it at one of his companions and struck him. He fell dead. Then the big man picked up the axe and looked at it for a moment and then threw it into the sea as far out as he could. Then they flee into the woods, whatever ways they can, and this meeting is over.

Karlsefni and his crew stayed on for the whole winter. But in springtime Karlsefni declares that he will stay there no longer, and will go to Greenland. They get ready from their voyage, and had a good cargo from the land, of grape-vines and grapes and fur pelts. They sail out to sea and brought their ship safe into Eirik's Firth and were there over the winter.

CHAPTER VII

Now talk about the Wineland voyage starts up again, because this voyage seems good for both wealth and fame.

That same summer a ship came from Norway to Greenland after Karlsefni got back from Wineland. This ship was captained by two brothers, Helgi and Finnbogi, and they stayed that winter in Greenland. These brothers were Icelanders and from the East Firths.

Now the story goes on that Freydis, Eirik's daughter, set out from Gardar and went to meet with the brothers, Helgi and Finnbogi, and asked them if they would come with her in their ship to Wineland and go halves with her on all the wealth that they might get there. So they agreed to this.

Then she went to see Leif her brother and asked him to give her the buildings that he had had built in Wineland. But he made the same answer, said he would lend the buildings but not give them.

This was the agreement between the brothers and Freydis, that each party should have 30 able-bodied men on their ship, and their women. But Freydis broke this at the beginning and had five men more and hid them, and the brothers did not know about them until they reached Wineland.

Now they put to sea, and first they had agreed that they would keep company if it could be done, and they were never far apart. But the brothers got in somewhat ahead, however, and had carried their gear up to Leif's buildings. And when Freydis and her crew arrived they unload their ship and carry their gear up to the buildings.

Then Freydis spoke: "Why did you put your gear in here?"

"Because we thought," say they, "that all agreements would hold between us."

"It was to me that Leif loaned the buildings," says she, "and not you."

Then Helgi spoke: "We brothers will hardly keep up with you in bad dealings." Then they took their gear out and made a building for themselves and put this building on the lakeshore further from the sea, and made it snug. And Freydis ordered timber to be felled for her cargo.

Now winter set in, and the brothers proposed that they should hold games and have some sport. So they did for a while, until people started behaving not so well. And then there was quarrelling between them, and the games were given up, and there was no coming and going between the buildings, and so it went on for long during the winter.

Then it was early one morning that Freydis got up out of her bed and got dressed and went out barefoot; and the weather was such that a heavy dew had fallen. She took her husband's cloak and put it on and then she went over to the brother's building and up to the doorway. A man had gone out a little before and slid the door halfway shut. She slid the door up and then stood at the threshold for a moment and said nothing. And Finnbogi lay furthest inside the building and he was awake.

He spoke: "What do you want over here, Freydis?"

She answers: "I want you to get up and go out with me, and I want to have a talk with you."

He does so. They go over to a log that lay by the wall of the building, and sit down on it.

"How do you like it here?" says she.

He answers: "I like what the land has to offer, but I do not like this bad feeling that is between us, because I reckon it was all started over nothing."

"It is as you say," says she, "and I feel the same; but my errand with you is this, that I want to barter ships with you brothers, because you have a larger ship than mine, and I want to get away from here."

"I shall agree to that," says he, "if that will please you."

Now they part. She goes home and Finnbogi goes to his bed. She gets up into bed with her cold feet and Thor-

34

vard wakes up from them and asks why she is so cold and wet.

She answers, very cross: "I had gone," says she, "to the brothers to bargain with them for their ship, for I wanted to buy the larger ship. But they got so ugly about it that they beat me, and manhandled me; but you are feeble and won't want to take vengeance either for my shame or yours, and now I can feel how far I am from Greenland, and I shall divorce myself from you unless you avenge this."

He could not bear her tongue any longer and told his men to get up quickly and take their weapons, and they do so, and go straight to the brothers' building and went in on them sleeping and seized them and tied them up. And Freydis had each killed as he came out.

Now all the men were killed and the women were left and nobody wanted to kill them.

Then Freydis spoke: "Hand me an axe."

They did.

Then she went at the five women who were there and killed them.

Now they went back to their building after this wicked deed, and from all that could be seen Freydis felt it had been well thought out and she spoke with her men: "If we are fated to get back to Greenland," says she, "I shall have that man dead who says anything about this business. Now, what we shall say is that they stayed on here when we went away."

Then they got their ship ready early in the spring, the one the brothers had owned, with all the freight that they could collect and the ship bear; sail out to sea then and had a good voyage and brought their ship into Eirik's Firth early in the summer. Karlsefni was there still and had got his ship all ready for sea and was waiting on a wind, and what men say is that there could not have been a richer ship depart from Greenland than the one he captained.

CHAPTER VIII

Freydis now went to her farm, which had stood untouched meanwhile. She handed over large portions of the take to all her crew, because she wanted her bad deeds kept quiet. Now she stays on her farm.

Everyone was not so close-mouthed that they could keep mum about their bad deeds and wickedness, so that word did not get out at last. Then it reached Leif her brother at last, and he thought it was the worst story.

Leif seized three of Freydis' crew and tortured stories of the whole business out of them and their stories all hung together.

"I have no heart," says Leif, "to deal with my sister Freydis as she deserves, but I shall foretell this for her and her husband, that their descendants will never come into much luck.

And after his words, no-one henceforth thought them

36

deserving of anything but bad.

Now there is this to tell, that Karlsefni got his ship ready and sailed out to sea. He had a good voyage and arrived in Norway safe and sound and stayed there over the winter and sold his cargo, and was much honoured there, both he and his wife, by the best born men in Norway. And the following spring he got his ship ready for Iceland.

And when he was all ready and his ship awaiting a favourable wind at the landing stage, up came a German to him, from Bremen in Saxony; he wants to bargain with Karlsefni for his ship's figurehead.

"I do not want to part with it," said he.

"I will give you half a mark of gold for it," says the German.

Karlsefni thought this a good offer, and they made the bargain. Off went the German with the figurehead, but Karlsefni did not know what kind of wood it was made of. But it was maple, and came from Wineland.

Now Karlsefni sails out to sea and brought his ship into the north of Iceland, in Skaga Firth, and his ship was laid up there for the winter. And in the spring he bought Glaumbyland and cleared a farm on it and lived there till the end of his life, and was a leading man in the country, and many men are descended from him and Gudrid his wife, a noble lineage.

And when Karlsefni died Gudrid managed the farm with Snorri, her son, who had been born in Wineland.

And when Snorri took a wife, Gudrid made the pilgrimage to Rome and came back out again to her son

Snorri's farm, and he had by then had a church built at Glaumby. Then Gudrid became a nun, an anchoress, and stayed there for the rest of her life.

Snorri had a son whose name was Thorgeir; he was the father of Yngvild, the mother of Bishop Brand. The daughter of Snorri Karlsefnisson was Hallfrid; she was the wife of Runolf, the father of Bishop Thorlak. Bjorn was a son of Karlsefni and Gudrid, he was the father of Thorunn, the mother of Bishop Bjorn.

Many men are descended from Karlsefni, and he has turned out to be a man fortunate in his family. And Karlsefni has told most fully of anyone about the events on all these voyages, which have been touched on here.

APPENDIX

Islendingabók

The land that is called Greenland was found and settled from Iceland. There was a man Eirik the Red from Broad Firth who went out there from here and took land there that has since been called Eirik's Firth. He named the land and called it Greenland and said that men would be keen to go there since the land had a good name. They found human dwellings both eastwards and westwards in the country, and remains of boats and stone tools from which it may be known that the kind of people had come there who had lived in Wineland, and the Greenlanders call skraelings.

And that time, when he went to settle the land, was fourteen or fifteen years before Christianity came here to Iceland, according to what a man told Thorkel Gellisson about Greenland, who had himself gone out with Eirik the Red.

Landnámabók (Sturlubók)

Thorvald the son of Asvald Wolfsson, the son of Thorir Ox, and Eirik the Red, his son, left Jaederen on acount of killings and took land at the Horn Strands and settled at Drangar. There died Thorvald. Eirik then married Thjodhild, the daughter of Jorund Atlason and Thorbjorg Ship-bosom, who was then married to Thorbjorn the Hawkdaler. Eirik then moved north and cleared land in Hawkdale. He lived at Eirik's Steading by Vatnshorn.

Then Eirik's thralls brought a landslip down on the farm of Valthjof of Valthjof's Steading, and Eyjolf Saur, his kinsman, killed the thralls at Skeithsbrekk up above Vatnshorn. For this Eirik killed Eyjolf Saur. He also killed Hrafn the Sworder at Leikskala.

Geirstein and Odd of Jarfa, Eyjolf's kinsmen, prosecuted the case for him. Then Eirik was driven out of Hawkdale. He then took Brok Island and Ox Island and lived at Tad on South Island the first winter. Then he loaned Thorgest his hall pillars.

Then Eirik moved to Ox Island and lived at Eirik's Steading. Then he claimed back his hall pillars but did not get them. Eirik went and fetched his hall pillars from Breidabol Steading, and Thorgest came after him. They fought a short way from the fence at Drangar. There fell two of Thorgest's sons and some other men.

After that both sides kept up their forces. Styrr stood with Eirik and also Eyjolf of Pig Island and the sons of Thorbrand from Swan Firth and Thorbjorn Vifilsson. But with Thorgest stood the sons of Roaring Thord and Thorgeir of Hotspring Dale, Aslak of Long Dale and Illugi, his son.

Eirik and his household were outlawed at Thorsness Thing.

He readied his ship in Eirik's Cove, and Eyjolf hid him

in Dimun Cove while Thorgest and his party were hunting for him among the islands. Thorbjorn and Eyjolf and Styrr went with Eirik out past the islands. He told them that he meant to look for the land that Gunnbjorn the son of Wolf Crow saw when he was driven west from Iceland, when he found Gunnbjorn's Skerries. He said he would come back to meet with his friends if he found the land.

Eirik set course from Snowfell's Glacier. And he made his landfall at Mid-Glacier, which is called Blue Sark. He turned south from there and coasted, to discover if there might be inhabitants that way. He stayed the first winter on Eirik's Island, near the middle of the Eastern Settlement.

Next spring he went to Eirik's Firth and took a steading for himself there. He journeyed that summer into the western wastes, and far and wide gave places their oldest names. He stayed the second winter on Eirik's Holm, by Hvarf's Peak. Again the third summer he went far north to Snowfell, and in to Raven's Firth. He declared that he had come inland opposite the head of Eirik's Firth. He turned back then and spent the third winter on Eirik's Island at the mouth of Eirik's Firth.

Then in the summer he sailed to Iceland and arrived in Broad Firth. He stayed that winter on Seal Island with Ingolf.

In the spring there was a fight with Thorgest and his men and Eirik was beaten. After that they made a settlement.

That summer Eirik went to live on the land he had

found and which he called Greenland, because he reckoned men would be very keen to go there if the land had a good name.

Wise men say that that summer there went 25 ships to Greenland from Broad Firth and Borg Firth and fourteen got there; some were driven back and some were lost. That was fifteen years before Christianity was received by law in Iceland. . . .

Then Eirik took Eirik's Firth and he lived at Brattahlid, and his son Leif after him.

These men took land in Greenland, who went out with Eirik: Herjulf took Herjulf's Firth—he lived on Herjulf's Ness—Ketil, Ketil's Firth; Hrafn, Hrafn's Firth; Solvi, Solvi's Dale; Helgi Thorbrandsson, Swan Firth; Thorbjorn Glora, Mast Firth; Einar, Einar's Firth; Hafgrim, Hafgrim's Firth and the Lake District; Arnlaug, Arnlaug's Firth. But some went to the Western Settlement.

NOTES

p 12: *"may his hawk's perch follow me"*   Hawk's perch was a kenning for hand or arm. A kenning was a poetic device for not calling a spade a spade but something else, often ingenious and far-fetched. It was common to all old Germanic poetry, but was most highly developed in the practice of the Icelandic skalds. In effect it was both riddling and metaphorical. The poet here is asking that the hand of God, the spotless monk-prover and Holy Master of high Heaven's Hall, may follow him, protectively.

p 19: *Wineland*   Whether *Vinland* should be translated *Wineland* or not is a question that has raised much discussion. It seems clear in this context of *The Greenlanders' Saga* that wine is what Leif means by *Vin*, but even here there are problems. The grapes must be wild and it does seem possible that they could have been growing in this part of Newfoundland at this time. Wild grapes will make good wine, but without much added sugar it will be weak and will probably turn to vinegar. The saga says nothing about wine except in the name *Wineland*. An unlikely circumstance is that the grapes were gathered and then kept over the winter and brought back to Greenland in the spring, so the wine, if there was any, must have been made from dried grapes. And vines were cut. What for? There seems to be no explanation

43

for this.

p 22: *"they came on a grain barn. . ."*   *Eirik the Red's Saga* and Adam of Bremen's *Gesta Hammaburgensis ecclesiae pontificum* both mention wild or "self-sown" grain in *Vinland. The Greenlanders' Saga* says nothing about wild grain, but it does bring this improbable *korn-hjálmr* into the story in a circumstantial way, as if it had been seen and told about in an early source. North American aborigines are not known to have stored grain at this time, and there have been many theories to explain this grain barn. Gathorne-Hardy thought it must have been a wigwam or some such dome-shaped abandoned dwelling that would remind the Norsemen of their own grain storage (see *Norse discoverers of America* [1970], p.48n).

p 23: *wattle*   The word translates *vigfleka*, which was a large defensive shield or shelter against stones and hurled missiles, made of sticks woven together. The English word wattle means interlaced sticks used in building, daubed with clay, or as a fence. As a dialect word it also means such an interlacing of sticks used defensively (see *OED*). It is not a familiar word, but it is exact, and I preferred it to an explanation incorporated into the text, which seemed the only alternative.

p 23: *"an arrow came. . ."*   The arrow suggests that the skraelings here must have been Indians, since the Eskimos in this area at this time did not use bows and arrows. An arrowhead was found at Sandness in Greenland by Aage

44

Roussell, exactly like an Indian arrowhead found at Lake Melville in Labrador. The arrowhead found in Greenland is made of the same sort of quartzite as occurs in Labrador (see Gwyn Jones, *The Norse Atlantic Saga,* p. 93).

p 27: *"illustrious and famous, sweet and of a good savour"*

Olafur Halldórsson conjectures that these words belong to the original saga, and underline its chief purpose, which was to tell the story of the illustrious forebears (Gudrid Thorbjornsdaughter and Thorfinn Karlsefni) of the illustrious Bishop Bjorn Gilsson. Shortly before 1200 the bones of Bishop Bjorn Gilsson and Bishop Jón Ogmundsson were dug up and washed, and people then waited to see which bishop would be most effective in working miracles. Jón Ogmundsson was showing himself rather more effective, but at the same time a life of Bjorn Gilsson was being undertaken, and it would be by this life that these words, which clearly refer to no ordinary bishops among Gudrid's descendants, would be inspired. Thorfinn and Gudrid's expedition is the most important matter in both Wineland sagas, and the effort to search out the facts for these sagas is probably connected with the competition in sanctity that involved their illustrious descendant.

p 30: *"a shadow fell across the doorway. . ."*   This encounter of Gudrid with her unearthly namesake is one of the more interesting and puzzling events in the saga. It is an awesome occasion, but its significance is obscure.

The namesake vanishes and at the same moment a skraeling is killed, the first instance of hostility between Thorfinn Karlsefni's party and the skraelings. There is no apparent connection between these two events, yet the story is told as if a connection is implied. Olafur Halldórsson has concluded that the unearthly woman is a *fylgja*, a following or guardian spirit, who would be most likely to appear to a man before his death. But the *fylgja* who appeared and spoke to Gudrid was, on the contrary, attaching herself to Gudrid's son Snorri at the beginning of his life. Olafur believes that she had been the *fylgja* of Snorri Thorbrandsson, whose death in Wineland is noted in *Eyrbyggja saga*. She must have left him when she knew he was doomed. Unaccountably, *The Greenlanders' Saga* makes no mention of him.

FURTHER READING

SOURCES (TRANSLATIONS INTO ENGLISH)

Adam of Bremen. Tschan, F. J. (translator). *History of the Archbishops of Hamburg-Bremen by Adam of Bremen*. New York: Columbia University Press, 1959.

Book of the Icelanders. Hermansson, H. (translator). *The Book of the Icelanders (Islendingabók) by Ari Thorgilsson*. Ithaca: Cornell University Press, 1930.

The Greenlanders' Saga and *Eirik the Red's Saga*. Magnússon, M. and Pálsson, H. (translators). *The Vinland Sagas*. London: Penguin Books, 1965.

GENERAL

Gathorne-Hardy, G. M. *The Norse Discoverers of America*. 1921. Re-issued in 1970 with a new preface by the author and a new introduction by Gwyn Jones.

Haugen, Einar. *Voyages to Vinland*. 1942.

Hovgaard, W. *The Voyages of the Norsemen to America*. 1914.

Ingstad, Helge. *Westward to Vinland*. 1965.

Jones, Gwyn. *The Norse Atlantic Saga*. 1964.

Reeves, A. M. *The Finding of Wineland the Good*. 1895.

ARTICLES

Ingstad, A. S. "The Norse Settlement at L'Anse-aux-Meadows, Newfoundland: A Preliminary Report from the Excavations 1961-68." *Acta Archaeologica*, XLI (1970), 109-54.

Ingstad, H. "Vinland Ruins Prove Vikings Found the New World." *National Geographic*, November 1964, pp. 708-34.

ABOUT THE VINLAND MAP

Crone, G. R. "How Authentic is the 'Vinland Map'?" *Encounter*, XXVI (1966), 75-78.

Foote, P. G. "On the Vinland Legends of *The Vinland Map*." *Saga Book of the Viking Society*, XVII. 73-89.

Skelton, R. A., Marston, T. E. and Painter, G. D. *The Vinland Map and the Tartar Relation*. New Haven: Yale University Press, 1970.

Symposium: Helen Wallis, F. R. Maddison, G. D. Painter, D. B. Quinn, R. M. Perkins, G. R. Crone, A. D. Baynes-Cope, Walter C. and Lucy B. McCrone, "The Strange Case of the Vinland Map." *Geographical Journal*, CXL. 2 (1974), 183-214.